More of
THE WORLD'S BEST DIRTY JOKES

<u>More</u> ribald.
<u>More</u> graphic.
<u>More</u> shocking.
<u>More</u> outrageous.
<u>More</u> hilarious.

More of
THE WORLD'S BEST DIRTY JOKES

Also by Mr. "J"
Published by Ballantine Books

THE WORLD'S BEST DIRTY JOKES

Mr. "J"

More of The World's Best Dirty Jokes

Illustrations by TED ENIK

BALLANTINE BOOKS · NEW YORK

Foreword

The stories and jokes in this collection are part and parcel of the folklore of America.

They are printed as they have been told, by word of mouth. In other times these jokes would have been subjected to stringent editing. Fortunately, today's mores permit almost limitless freedom of expression.

And we are all the richer for it.

Allen was sitting at a bar in a Miami Beach hotel feeling exceedingly horny, when a beautiful prostitute approached him.

"How much do you want?" asked Allen.

"One hundred dollars for the evening," said the prostitute.

"Well, if I'm going to pay that kind of money, you must do it under my rules."

She said, "Honey, that's fine, as long as you're paying."

Allen said, "Okay, meet me in my room in ten minutes and we'll close the drapes, turn out the lights, and do it in pitch-black darkness."

"That's okay, honey. It's your money."

When they got together in the room, Allen really gave it to her. Then he said, "Let's rest a few moments," and then he started in again. The same scene was played for two hours. Finally, after six encounters, Allen seemed even stronger than before.

The prostitute said, "Allen you are the most fantastic lover I have ever had. You just keep getting better and better."

"Listen, lady," said a voice. "My name is Herman. Allen is outside selling your ass to his friends at fifty bucks a throw."

Definition of a diaphragm: a trampoline for schmucks.

As Adam wandered about the Garden of Eden, he noticed two birds up in a tree. They were snuggled up together, billing and cooing.

Adam called to the Lord, "What are the two birds doing in the trees?"

The Lord said, "They are making love, Adam."

A little while later he wandered into the fields and saw a bull and a cow going at it hot and heavy. He called to the Lord, "Lord, what's going on with that bull and cow?"

And the Lord said, "They're making love, Adam."

Adam said, "How come I don't have anyone to make love with?"

So the Lord said, "We'll change that. When you awake tomorrow morning things will be different."

So Adam lay down beneath the olive tree and fell asleep. When he awoke, there was Eve next to him. Adam jumped up, grabbed her hand, and said, "Come with me. Let's go into the bushes." And so they went.

But a few moments later Adam stumbled out, looking very dejected, and called to the Lord, "Lord, what's a headache?"

A New York dress manufacturer, specializing in the production of pastel dresses, had signs pasted in the washrooms: YOU ARE WORKING ON PASTELS! EMPLOYEES MUST WASH HANDS AFTER USING THE LAVATORY.

Two workers, buttoning their flies as they emerged from the washroom, were queried by the boss: "Did you wash your hands? You're working on pastels."

"Nah," replied one worker. "We're not working on pastels. We're going to lunch!"

A patient at Mount Sinai Hospital, recovering from minor surgery, was being given an alcohol rubdown by two of the hospital's more attractive nurses. While manipulating the man's body they noted that the word *tiny* was tattooed on the head of his penis.

Some months after the man's discharge, Mary, one of the nurses, told Joan, the other, that she had dated their former patient.

"How could you go out with a man who had 'tiny' tattooed on his love stick?" exclaimed Joan.

"How could I indeed!" said Mary. "It said 'tiny' when it was quiet, but when I aroused it, it spelled out 'Tiny's Delicatessen and Catering Service. We deliver at all times, twenty-four hours a day!' "

An inventor, seeking a loan from a bank, told his banker that he'd discovered a remarkable substance that, brushed lightly over a lady's pussy, would give it an orange flavor.

"No good," the banker responded, after some thought. "But if you can invent something to put into an orange that will make it taste like pussy, you can have your loan and we'll both get rich!"

A shy young man, preparing himself for what he hoped would be the ultimate sex act with a pretty young lady, went into a drugstore to inquire about sizes and styles of condoms.

The lusty proprietress, a buxom widow, saw an opportunity for fun at the lad's expense.

"Come in the back and try some on for size," she said, taking his hand. The widow unzipped the youth's fly and watched the small instrument grow in her hand as she measured it. When the weapon had unfurled to a rosy seven and a half inches, the young man, unable to contain himself, had an orgasm with a tremendous discharge. After recovering, he asked the widow if she could now give him the proper size.

"I'll do more than that," she said. "I'll give you free meals and a one-half interest in the store."

I'm so tired," complained the pretty young actress to her friend. "Last night I didn't sleep until after three."

"No wonder you're tired," her friend replied. "Twice is usually all I need."

A happily married man, Irving Topper, found himself driving through a badly paved country road in upstate Rhinebeck, New York. A sudden flat tire sent the car wobbling to a standstill.

The lights in a nearby health manor invited Topper to rap on the door. An attractive lady opened the door and asked what she could do for him. He told her his problem and wondered if he could seek the shelter of her house until dawn, when he would repair the flat. The lady agreed and invited him into her parlor.

One word led to another; one drink led to another; one touch led to another. Irving Topper was soon divested of his clothes and snuggling in the lady's bed with an equally naked lady.

In the morning Topper thanked her for her hospitality, told her his name was Herman Thompson, changed his tire, and drove off.

About six months later, Topper received a call from his friend Herman Thompson.

"Hey," said Thompson, "did you ever give my name to a lady in Rhinebeck, New York?"

"Well, yes," answered Topper. "You know I am a married man, and I have a lovely wife and child. I gave her your name because you're a bachelor, and I didn't want any complications. I hope I didn't get you into any trouble."

"No, no, on the contrary," replied his friend. "Her

10

lawyer called me to inform me that I had inherited the manor and the lady's entire estate!"

A painter, whitewashing the inner walls of a country outhouse, had the misfortune to fall through the opening and land in the muck at the bottom. He shouted, "Fire! Fire! Fire!" at the top of his lungs.

The local fire department responded with alacrity, sirens roaring as they approached the privy.

"Where's the fire?" called the chief.

"No fire," replied the painter as they pulled him out of the hole. "But if I had yelled, 'Shit! Shit! Shit!' who would have rescued me?"

A seventy-five-year-old gentleman visited his doctor to complain about his impotency.

"Why me?" he grumbled. "I have a friend eighty years old who says that he—"

The doctor interrupted: "You can *say* too!"

Bendelman, a top salesman for a wholesale hardware company, was traveling on one of his quarterly selling swings. When he arrived in Indianapolis he was caught in a blizzard of awesome proportions. At the end of the day he was happy to seek the warmth of his hotel room. One of his major accounts found the snow so heavy that he felt he could not drive to his suburban home. He asked Bendelman if he could put him up for the night in his room, since the hotel was full.

Bendelman, knowing that the man was one of his best accounts, glady offered to share his double-bedded room. After a good dinner and ample liquor they repaired for the night. In the middle of the night Bendelman felt a hand on his privates. Possibly his companion was dreaming. But there was no mistaking his intent when an erect penis brushed against his lips.

When Bendelman returned home he told his wife the story. "And what did you do?" she asked.

"What could I do?" sighed Bendelman, "He was my best account in Indianapolis."

An eminent teacher and thinker once expressed his philosophy of life succinctly. "When it all boils down to the essence of truth," the philosopher said, "one must live by a dog's rule of life: If you can't eat it or fuck it, piss on it!"

A.___ B.___ C.___

The young farm helper was telling his friend about his wedding night.

"Boy, was my girl dumb! She put a pillow under her ass instead of her head."

Two friends decided they would beat the draft by having all their teeth pulled. They knew the army would not take them if they were toothless.

Finally the day came when they were to report to the draft board. As they lined up they were separated by a big truck driver who obviously had not bathed for weeks. When the first friend stood before the sergeant for a physical examination he told the sergeant that he had no teeth. The sergeant ran his fingers around the man's gums and said, "All right, you have no teeth— you're 4F."

Next came the big, smelly truck driver. The sergeant said, "What's wrong with you?"

The truck driver replied, "I have a terrible case of piles."

The sergeant inserted his fingers in the truck driver's ass, felt around, and said, "Yes, indeed you do; you're 4F."

Next came the second friend, and the sergeant said, "What's wrong with you?"

The recruit stared at the sergeant's finger. "Nothing, Sergeant," he said. "Nothing at all."

Mrs. Anderson's husband had been reported missing for more than three months. Her friends and relatives did not know if the poor man had met with foul play or had merely absented himself from the family hearth.

One day the lady received a call from the city morgue requesting her to identify a body that might very well be Mr. Anderson.

The morgue attendant lifted the sheet, disclosing the recently dead but very well-endowed corpse.

"No," Mrs. Anderson said. "That isn't my husband, but some woman certainly lost a very good friend."

Marty was walking down the street when he saw his friend and yelled to him, "John, how are you?"

John replied, "Don't call me John. Call me Lucky."

"Why should I call you Lucky?"

John proceeded to tell him that he had been standing on the corner of 52nd Street and Third Avenue, when he stepped off the curb just as a two-ton safe fell from the twentieth floor. It landed right where he had been standing an instant earlier.

Marty said, "My God, you certainly are lucky. That will be your name from now on."

A few weeks later they bumped into each other again, and Marty said, "Lucky, how are you?"

To which came the reply, "Don't call me Lucky. Call me Lucky, Lucky."

Marty said, "Tell me now, why I should call you Lucky, Lucky?" and was told that Lucky had been bumped from a flight to Miami that was later hijacked to Cuba.

Marty agreed, "You certainly are Lucky, Lucky."

The next time they met, Marty shouted, "Lucky, Lucky, how are you?"

To which the reply was, "Don't call me Lucky, Lucky. Call me Lucky, Lucky, Lucky."

Marty said, "Why?"

Lucky, Lucky, Lucky said, "Just last week I took

my girlfriend to a hotel room for a matinee, and we made such a commotion that the chandelier over the bed came down and landed right on her cunt."

Marty said, "But what's so lucky about that?"

To which came the reply, "Ten seconds earlier, it would have cut off my head."

Three words guaranteed to destroy any man's ego: "Is it in?"

The Pope had been sick for a number of months, and experts were called in from all over the world, but no one could diagnose his illness. Finally a doctor from Switzerland came and immediately hit upon the cause of the problem.

He said to the Pope, "Your Holiness, because you have lived in a celibate state all your life, your seminal fluids have built up and are literally choking you to death. Therefore, there is only one cure. You must have sexual intercourse with a woman!"

The Pope cried out in dismay, "But I can't. I *can't!* You know the vows I have taken. I just cannot."

The doctor replied, "But Your Holiness, if you don't do this you will condemn yourself to death. This, too, is a mortal sin."

The Pope pondered the problem and said, "I will retire to my room for three days of prayer, and then I will make a decision."

At the end of the three days he telephoned the doctor in Switzerland and said, "My decision has been made. I will do what you direct. But please be sure that she has big tits!"

A young whore, after banging some thirty men in the course of the evening, died and was taken to the great Olympia in the sky. There she met the god Thor, who immediately made a pass at her.

"You cannot reject me," he exclaimed. "I'm Thor!"

"*You're* thor," she mimicked. "After thirty guys in a row, I'm the one who's sore!"

A father was talking to his son just before the son's marriage, explaining what the son could be looking forward to in his marriage.

He said, "Son, in the very beginning, it's triweekly. After you've been married ten years or so, it's try weekly. But then after your silver anniversary, it's try weakly."

The priest at Sunday mass noticed that Michael took a ten-dollar bill and two one-dollar bills from the collection plate, instead of putting something in. He thought to himself, *I'd better watch out for Michael.*

The next week he noticed the same thing. So he waited outside church when mass was over, and as Michael came out, he accosted him and said, "Michael, tell me—why did you take out a ten-dollar bill and two singles two weeks in a row, instead of putting money into the collection?"

Michael replied, "Father, I'm embarrassed, but I did it because I needed a blow job."

The priest looked surprised but said to Michael, "Listen, don't do that any more. I'll be watching you from now on."

When he got back to the rectory, the priest was still perplexed. Finally he decided to call Mother Agatha at the convent. He said, "Mother, you've been such a great friend of mine, I have a question for you. What is a blow job?"

Mother Agatha replied, "Oh, about twelve dollars."

The famous Yiddish actor Boris Tomashefsky was celebrated for his bedroom exploits as well as his stage virtuosity. After a sexual bout with a local whore, he presented her with a pair of tickets to the evening performance of his play.

The lady looked with skepticism at the tickets. "With these you can buy bread?" she asked.

"If you're looking for bread," the actor said, "screw a baker."

A husband, returning home unexpectedly, found his wife on her hands and knees scrubbing the kitchen floor. The piston-like movement of her buttocks, encased in a sheer dressing gown, sent a message to his brain.

Without a by-your-leave, he lifted her gown, unzipped himself, and proceeded to mount her.

After they had sighed in mutual satisfaction, the wife resumed her task. This time he booted her in the behind.

"Is that nice, Sam, kicking me after I gave you so much pleasure?"

"That," he said, "is for not looking to see who it was!"

It's a business doing pleasure with you," said the whore as she accepted her payment.

LM. Goldman, a traveling representative for a brush company, covered the entire eastern seaboard. Each day he would send the home office an itemized column of expenses for that day. He would list food, transportation, and hotel charges, and at the bottom of each page of expenditures he would add, "5.00—a man isn't made of wood."

When the home office received seven consecutive similar notations they cabled Goldman: "It's true a man isn't made of wood, but he isn't made of steel, either!"

A man, very much on the make for his secretary, wined her and dined her. He finally succeeded in getting her to his apartment, where he whispered sweet promises into her ear while he began to unbutton her blouse.

"If we get together," he said, "a fur coat . . . perhaps a trip to Europe."

The secretary nodded a cheerful agreement, and soon the two were locked in intercourse. Later, while dressing, she asked him when she could get the fur coat he'd promised.

"What fur coat?" he asked.

"You promised me a fur coat," she said.

"When I'm horny I'll promise anything," he said. Putting one hand on his heart and one on his sexual organ, he added, "When he's soft, he's hard. When he's hard, he's soft."

A whore and her pimp were lounging in her hotel room, when she got a call from a customer. The pimp, despite the frigid weather outside, offered to wait out on the balcony while the whore did her work.

The customer turned up in ten minutes and was soon humping the whore under the warm blanket. A half hour later, refreshed and satisfied, the customer left.

The pimp, shivering, his lips blue from the biting cold and icicles on his ears, returned to the room and called, "Has that sucker gone yet?"

Jessie James and his gang attacked a train just outside Oklahoma City. They went through each car lining up the travelers and preparing to take all the loot they could handle.

Jessie entered the first car and yelled, "Okay, everybody, we're going to rape all the men and rob all the women."

His brother Frank turned to him and said, "Jessie, we're going to rob all the men and rape all the women."

With that, a little fairy in the corner piped up, "Listen, you heard Jessie. He's the boss."

A young salesman visited a whorehouse in Kansas City and proceeded to give the blonde prostitute the greatest lay she had ever experienced.

"Listen," she said, "if you can repeat that performance, I'll give it to you for nothing."

The salesman said, "Okay, but let me rest for ten minutes. But while I do, to help recharge my batteries, just sit here and hold my cock." After ten minutes, he gave it to her again, and it was more wonderful than the first time.

When they were through, the excited prostitute said, "Please, let's do it again. You can have it for nothing."

The salesman said, "Okay, just give me another ten-minute rest and sit here holding my cock."

She said, "Of course." Then she said, "Listen, I can understand your wanting that ten-minute rest, but why do you have me sit here holding your cock?"

"Because in St. Louis, the last prostitute I visited stole my wallet!"

Then there's the story of the man who was standing on Delancey Street gazing at his watch, which was obviously not working. He spied a corner shop which had a gigantic clock in the window. Thinking it was a watch-repair shop, he approached the owner and said, "My watch doesn't work; please fix it for me."

The owner said, "I'm not a watchmaker. I'm a *mohel*."*

The man replied, "Then why do you have the big clock in your window?"

Said the shopkeeper, "What would you put in your window?"

* *Mohel:* Yiddish, one who circumcises.

The bride-to-be and her best friend were discussing the former's impending wedding.

"If you want an unforgettable wedding night," her friend said, "get him to eat a dozen oysters after the ceremony."

A week later the new bride thanked her friend but said plaintively, "Only eight of the oysters worked."

The famous stage magician had a thundering climax to his act. He would fill a large bowl with shit and proceed to slurp it noisily, to the amazement and delight of the audience.

One evening he had just begun the wow finish of the act when he stopped in his tracks.

"Go ahead," murmured the stage manager. "Eat the shit. Eat it!"

"Can't do it," said the magician. "There's a hair in it!"

An American soldier, on the train from London to Liverpool, shared a compartment with two English brothers, one of whom was hard of hearing. They struck up a conversation, and one brother said, "I say, Yank, where are you going?"

"Liverpool," said the American.

"What did he say?" asked the hard-of-hearing brother.

"He said he's going to Liverpool. Tell me, Yank. what brings you all the way to Liverpool?"

"I have a girlfriend up there."

"What did he say?" asked the hard-of-hearing brother again.

"He said he has a girlfriend there. She must be quite a girl if you'll travel all the way there just to see her."

"I'll say she is!" said the American. "She wears black boots with spurs, carries a whip, and indulges in every delight known to man."

"What did he say?" asked the brother who was hard of hearing.

"He said he knows Mother."

The Smiths had been married long enough for the bloom to be off the rose. Yet from time to time Smith was overcome by the primal urge. On one such occasion, while they were sitting in the living room before the television set, Smith nudged his wife and said, "How about going into the bedroom?"

"No," said Mrs. Smith.

Smith finally persuaded her to change her mind. She disrobed for bed and donned a long nightgown.

"Pull up the nightgown, honey," he requested.

"No," said Mrs. Smith.

Just then the front-door bell rang, and Smith pulled on a robe to answer it. Mrs. Smith immediately leaped from the bed and bolted the bedroom door.

The irate Smith banged on the door and yelled, "Let me in . . . let me in! If you don't unlock the door, I'll break it down."

"Look at him," Mrs. Smith said. "He can't even lift a nightgown, and he's talking about breaking down doors!"

It's very simple," explained the go-go dancer. "First I kick my right foot; then I kick my left foot. Between the two of them, I make a living."

In the romantic days of Warsaw, Viennese whores were known for their beauty and delicacy. A gallant officer picked up one such lady of the evening, who took him to her apartment. They made delicious love all evening before drifting to sleep in each other's arms. In the morning the man dressed, staring into a full-length mirror. The lady lay in her bed watching him.

Finally she said softly, "Didn't you forget something?"

"What did I forget?" asked the officer.

"You forgot about money," said the lady.

"Oh, no," said the man, standing at ramrod attention. "A Polish officer never takes money."

om's dream was to marry a sweet, innocent virgin. He'd been going with Jane for a few months, when he decided to test her. As they drove along in the car, he unzipped his fly, turned to her, and said, "Do you want to see my wee-wee?"

She yelled, "No! No! Please zip up your fly."

Instead of being annoyed, Tom was pleased.

On the evening of their engagement to be married, he tried the same thing, with the same result. Finally, on their wedding night, they were alone in the hotel room when he unzipped his fly and said to her, "Darling, now you can look at what I've got here," and proceeded to take out his organ.

She looked at it and replied, "Oh, what a sweet looking wee-wee!"

Tom said, "No, darling—you don't have to call it a wee-wee now; you can call it a cock."

She looked at it for a while and then said, "No, Tom, that's a wee-wee. A cock is long and thick and black."

And then there's the little boy who got up at midnight to go to the bathroom and passed his parents' bedroom. Noticing that the door was opened, he walked in and saw his mother performing fellatio on his father.

The boy walked out of the bedroom scratching his head and muttering, "And they sent *me* to the doctor for sucking my thumb!"

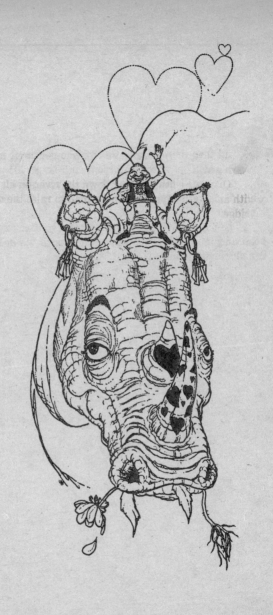

What are the two most conceited things in the world?

One is the flea, floating down the river on his back with an erection, yelling for the man to raise the drawbridge.

The other is the flea's brother who, after sexually attacking a rhinoceros, whispers in her ear, "Did I hurt you, baby?"

he eminent physician was at a loss on how to proceed with treatment for his hypochondriac patient. The man had been consulting with him for months; yet the doctor could find nothing wrong with him.

Finally, the doctor decided to bring matters to a head. This time he gave the patient a large bowl and ordered him to urinate in it. The patient followed orders. Then the doctor ordered him to defecate in the urine. It was difficult but the patient complied.

The physician took a large wooden ladle from a drawer and mixed the concoction. Then he ordered the patient to open his mouth and swallow a large ladleful of the muck. The patient did so and promptly vomited.

"Ah!" said the doctor. "Upset stomach!"

businessman returned home from the office with some startling gossip. He informed his wife that he'd heard that their neighbor in apartment 4-G had fucked every woman in the building except one.

"That's right," replied the wife. "It's that stuck-up Mrs. Cohen on the eighth floor!"

The parlormaid in the home of a famous acting family was openly desired and admired by the nineteen-year-old son of the household. He schemed and schemed but could think of no way to get the young woman into his bed.

Finally, one evening, opportunity presented itself and he persuaded the young miss to join him between the sheets. Much to his despair and chagrin, his weapon refused to come to attention.

"Don't feel too bad," the parlormaid said. "The same thing often happens to your father."

The Adamses, celebrating their twenty-fifth wedding anniversary, decided to recapture their nuptial night by making love the way they had when they first discovered sex with each other. Mr. Adams perspired until he achieved a serviceable erection, and then began to put it to its proper use.

Mrs. Adams, bouncing under her husband's weight, never took her eyes off the window.

"Darling," she murmured, just as he felt the tickle of approaching orgasm, "should we redo this room with cream curtains or a pretty print?"

Bumper stickers observed:

MECHANICS HAVE THE BEST TOOLS.
LOVE THE NAVY—EAT A SAILOR TODAY!
DON'T BE HALF-GAY.
SMILE . . . IF YOU WERE LAID LAST NIGHT!
JOURNALISTS DO IT EVERY DAY.

John had two pet monkeys whom he loved very much, but both died within two days of each other. He decided to take their bodies to the taxidermist so that they would be with him forever. The taxidermist gave him an estimate for the job and asked if he wanted them mounted.

"No," came the reply. "Just have them shaking hands."

The absent-minded professor unbuttoned his vest, took out his necktie, and wet his pants.

A young black guy, traveling cross-country with his girlfriend, left her alone in a hotel room while he visited a local bar for a few drinks. When he returned, he found his girl snoring contentedly in bed, limbs sprawled askew. The sound of his stropping a straight razor awakened her.

"What are you gonna do with the razor?" she asked.

Continuing his methodic stropping as he stared at two rolled up towels in the sink, he said, "I'm gonna give myself a shave . . . if these two towels dry soft!"

John had been at the university for more than two years, and his grades had gradually become worse. His father called the dean to find out why.

"Well," the dean replied, "I have good news and I have bad news. Your son is in such poor shape with his school work because he has become a blatant homosexual and does nothing but pursue the boys on the football and basketball teams."

"My God, that's awful!" replied the father. "Tell me quickly, what is the good news?"

The dean replied, "He's been voted Queen of the May."

A bosomy blonde was trying on an extremely low-cut dress. As she studied herself in the mirror, she asked the saleswoman if she thought it was too low-cut.

"Do you have hair on your chest?" the saleswoman asked.

"No!"

"Then," the saleswoman said, "it's too low-cut!"

Once upon a time there was a little sperm. He lived with many thousands of other little sperm, but this little sperm was different. He dreamed endlessly of the glorious day (or night, most likely) when he and his friends would be released to accomplish their great mission in life. The man they inhabited, however, practiced coitus interruptus, and at the moment of orgasm, the small army found itself denied release.

One night, the little sperm told his pals: "Enough of this! The next time he arrives at the point of orgasm, let's make a concentrated rush."

The big moment arrived, but one of the vanguard yelled: "Back up! Back up! He's in the asshole!"

Correct social behavior: In the Catskill resorts couples often share rooms with other couples. Because of this, they frequently indulge in lovemaking under the stars. Should someone happen to step on a recumbent pair, the one stepped on usually says, "Thank you!"

Two hunters were in the woods miles and miles from civilization, when the one had to take a crap. He went into the bushes, but came out screaming, "Joe, Joe, please—While I was in the bushes a snake came and bit the tip of my prick. Please, please, you have to suck out the venom."

To which Joe replied, "Baby, you're going to die!"

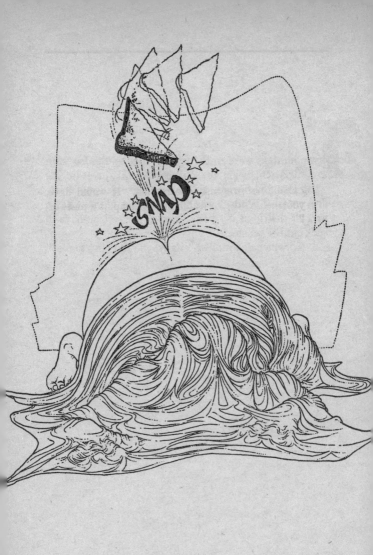

A patient at a local hospital was being fed rectally. When a relative of the patient asked his nurse about his progress, she replied, "It would have done your heart good to watch his ass snap at a piece of toast!"

A salesman was driving along a lonely stretch of Interstate 95 in a heavy rainstorm, when he spied a hitchhiker. He stopped and picked him up. As they proceeded on their way, the salesman explained that he very rarely picked up a hitchhiker, but the storm was so bad he just had to stop for this man.

The hitchhiker then asked why the salesman did not make it a practice to pick up people on the road. The salesman said, "Well, I used to, until one day when my wife and I picked up a hitchhiker who pulled a gun on us, took our money and clothes, and made my wife get in the back seat and suck him off."

"Well, darling," came the effeminate voice of the hitchhiker, as he pulled his gun, "this just isn't your day."

A young man was extolling the virtues of his beautiful fiancée. One of his closest friends exclaimed, "You can't be serious about marrying Sarah Jane! Why, she's fucked every man in Syracuse."

The bridegroom-to-be thought awhile and then muttered pensively, "Syracuse isn't such a big town."

Two friends, during a pleasurable walk, were engaged in a friendly dispute over the question as to which afforded the greater joy—sexual intercourse or moving the bowels.

As they walked along, a call girl, familiar to both, appeared in their path.

"Let us ask her opinion," said one friend. "She is well experienced in both functions."

The other objected, "She's not the one for an impartial answer. She has slept with men much more frequently than she's been to the john."

Persuasion was necessary, but the amorous swain had finally gotten his girlfriend between the sheets. In due course he made love to her, finally burying his sword in her sheath and beginning to screw away.

"Be careful," she panted. "I think I have a weak heart."

"Don't worry," he said, without missing a stroke. "I'll take it very easy when I get up to the heart!"

A prominent television writer was being ministered to by a talented whore, who was giving him a total body tongue job, more commonly known as a trip around the world. At the same time he was arguing on the telephone with a collaborator over a plot twist on a new television drama on which they were working jointly. The argument got so heated that the whore looked up from her work and complained, "For Christ's sake, argue on your own time."

The writer bellowed into the phone, "We're going to do it my way!" And then he turned to the girl. "And you . . . you keep a civil tongue in my ass!"

Two ladies of easy virtue were comparing notes at a Las Vegas hotel poolside. "The man I go with gave me two hundred dollars yesterday," said one.

"Gross?" asked the other.

"No, his name was Schwartz."

An archaeologist, studying a calcified substance he discovered in one of the pharaoh's tombs, somberly presented his findings to the commission. "It is my studied opinion," he said, "that a cat crept into the crypt, crapped, and then crept out again."

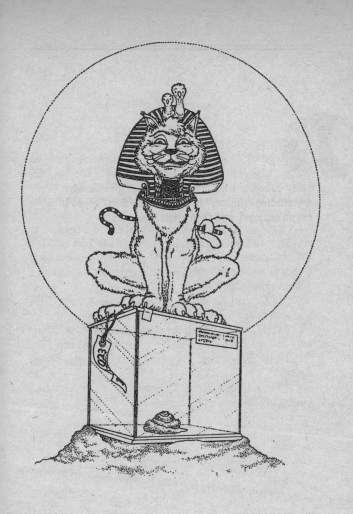

Diane was a beautiful girl. As she was walking down the lane one hot summer's day, the heat became so unbearable that she decided to go for a swim. She took off her clothes, piled them neatly on the side of the riverbank, and dived in.

A couple of young boys came along and decided to steal her clothes. It grew dark, and Diane just couldn't stay in the water any longer, so she went to the side of the road and decided to hitch a ride home. Along came Mike, riding a bicycle.

He stopped for Diane. "Come," he said. "I'll drive you into town." She jumped on his bicycle.

Mike said nothing, but after ten minutes Diane was so overwhelmed at how cool he was that she said, "Tell me, haven't you noticed that I'm completely naked?"

"Sure," said Mike. "Haven't you noticed that you're riding on a girl's bicycle?"

Sam Cohen was making himself comfortable in Dimples' room in Madame Olga's whorehouse, when the place was suddenly overrun by the police in a surprise raid. As Sam ran down the stairs he zipped up his fly. When he reached the front door he met Irving, a friend and fellow garment manufacturer.

As he headed for his automobile, he yelled, "When the cops disappear, go up to the third floor and throw Dimples a bang. It's paid for!"

A tall, two-hundred-pound Texan, who was a loud braggart, died suddenly of a heart attack. At the funeral services his friends were surprised to note the small size of the coffin.

"That can't be what's left of Big Tom Gallagher," said one of his friends.

"Sure it is!" replied another mourner. "They simply let the bullshit out of him."

B elle Barth talked about a bride who was celebrating the first night of her third honeymoon. Presenting herself as a virgin, she kept crying, "It hurts, it hurts!" while her new husband struggled to twine his feet around the bedpost to keep from falling in.

In desperation, the young bride finally took pen in hand and wrote to Xaviera Hollander:

> I'm married to a sex maniac. My husband never leaves me alone. He makes love to me all night long—while I'm in the shower, while I'm cooking breakfast, while I'm making the beds, and even while I'm trying to clean the house. Can you tell me what to do?
>
> Signed,
Worn Out
>
> P.S. Please excuse the jerky handwriting.

A young couple were out on a date, attending a concert. The auditorium was pitch dark and, as lovers will, they began to fondle each other. After a while she felt something wet and sticky and realized the boy had come in her hand. She panicked for a moment and then, figuring it was too dark for anyone to see what she was doing, flung the stuff as far in front of her as she could.

It hit the second violinist on the shoulder. He felt something hit him and, trying to get it off, realized what it was.

"Hey," he whispered to the first violinist, "someone just threw me a fuck."

"I'm not surprised," snarled the first violinist. "You've been playing like a cunt all night!"

When queried by his best friend about the joys of his recent marriage, the young bridegroom shook his head disconsolately.

"I'm not sure," he muttered. "When I planned marriage I had dreams of a girl who'd be a lady in the streets, a great cook in the kitchen, and a *nafkeh* [whore] in bed. And what do I have? A *nafkeh* in the streets, a lady in the bedroom, and a great cook . . . never!"

The third-grade teacher was conducting a class in nutrition and asked the class to name four qualities of mother's milk.

Jimmy said, "I know, teacher. Number one, it's fresh. Number two, it's nutritious. Number three, it's served at just the right temperature. And number four, it comes in such a cute little container."

Sam, from the garment center in New York, went to Miami Beach for a winter vacation. While walking down Collins Avenue, he was approached by a luscious blonde, who whispered into his ear, "I'm selling—are you buying?"

Sam said, "Sure, I'm buying."

So they went to a hotel room and made love for the entire night.

A week or so later, when Sam went back to New York, he came down with syphilis. After weeks and weeks of painful treatment, Sam was released by the hospital. As he was walking along Fifth Avenue, the same blonde came over to him and whispered, "I'm selling, mister—are you buying?"

Sam looked her straight in the eye and asked, "So what are you selling now, cancer?"

A dry-goods buyer for a department-store chain was making his annual tour of the mills, searching for fresh merchandise. His trip lasted longer than usual, but he kept in touch with his wife by wiring her nightly: "Still traveling, still buying." After ten days of such wires the wife telegraphed him back: "Come home at once or I'll be selling what you're buying!"

An actor who had drunk too much vodka was faced with the need for instant sobriety. Drinking coffee usually took too long to sober him, but the actor's physician came to the rescue by suggesting a coffee enema as a quick and sure method. The actor agreed and submitted.

As the doctor's nurse was administering the enema he yelled, "Hey! What brand are you using?"

"Maxwell House."

"Forget it," said the actor. "It's the one brand I can't drink."

The stout prostitute disrobed and spread out on the bed awaiting her customer, a newly beached sailor. In his anxiety to relieve his passion he found the wrong opening while poking beneath the rolls of fat.

"You're in the wrong hole!" she screamed.

"Any port in a storm," said the sailor, pressing on.

Belle Barth told the story of the sweet young thing who was taken to a fancy East Side restaurant in New York by her elderly employer. After a few cocktails, the young lady ordered a pâté de foie gras, an endive salad, chateaubriand, and dessert and coffee. She did not omit a fine wine.

The old gentleman stared quizzically at her: "Your mother feeds you this way?" he asked.

"No," replied the sweet young thing, "but my mother's not looking to fuck me, either!"

Giovanni lived in Palermo, Italy. One day he arrived from work early, to find his wife in bed with Pietro, the butcher.

The wife screamed; Pietro screamed.

Meanwhile, Giovanni ran to the closet, pulled out a pistol, and faced his wife.

He put the barrel of the pistol to his forehead and smirked at her: "Don't feel sorry for me, you bitch. You're gonna be next!"

The bright young man working in the produce section of a large supermarket in Detroit was approached by a customer.

"I want half a head of lettuce," the man said.

"Sir, we can't sell half a head of lettuce," the young clerk explained.

The man persisted and the young man agreed to check with the store's manager.

He found the manager and said, "Mr. Peterson, I've got some nut in the produce department who wants to buy half a head of lettuce." Just as he finished his statement he saw that the customer had followed him and was standing next to him. "And this gentleman," he said hastily, "wants to buy the other half."

"Sell it," the manager said.

Later, the manager took the youth aside. "That was quick thinking," he said. "We need bright young men like you, and I'm going to keep my eyes open on your behalf."

"Thanks, Mr. Peterson," the young man said.

Two weeks later he was summoned by the manager.

"Well, my lad, I told you I'd watch out for you, and indeed I have. I've recommended you for an assistant manager's job in our new store in Montreal—"

"Montreal!" the young man exclaimed. "Why,

nothing comes from there except hookers and hockey players!"

Peterson said, "Listen, young fellow, my wife comes from there!"

Without missing a beat, the young man replied, "No kidding! What position does she play?"

There was a hurried inspection call at the marine base in Camp Lagoon. Most of the marines were caught in bed naked and had no time to dress, so they lined up outside the barracks shivering and nude. As the marine sergeant went down the line, he saw one of the recruits with an impressive hardon. He walked up to it and gave it a vicious swat with his club. Expecting the recruit to be doubed over in pain, the sergeant was amazed that he stood there with a big smile on his face.

He exclaimed to the recruit, "My God, I can't believe it. I just swatted your penis, and you stand there and smile back at me."

The recruit answered, "I'm smiling because the cock belongs to the man behind me."

Two business partners, both married, were taking turns having intercourse with their attractive secretary. As a result of such frequent fucking, the young lady became pregnant with twins.

One partner, congratulating the other, said, "Susie had twins. Unfortunately, mine died!"

George took his girlfriend to bed for the first time. He was working away very hard, but she was not responding at all. Finally, in exasperation, he asked her, "What's the matter?"

She said: "It's your organ. I don't think it's big enough."

To which George replied, "Well, I didn't think I'd be playing in a cathedral!"

Jones, returning from a business trip, was surprised to find his wife in bed with a strange man. The stranger, nude and obviously well satisfied, was sprawled over the bed.

"Why, you rotten bastard!" the husband exploded.

"Wait, darling," said Mrs. Jones. "You know that fur coat I got last winter? This man gave it to me. Remember the diamond necklace you like so much? This man gave it to me. And remember when you couldn't afford a second car and I got a Toyota? This man gave it to me."

"For heaven's sake, it's drafty here!" shouted the husband "Cover him so he doesn't catch cold!"

A wealthy Jewish lawyer was unhappy over the romantic pursuits of his junior-college son. He told his closest friend, "My son's a homosexual." But then he added, "The situation could be worse, though. He's in love with a doctor."

Jim and Tom were sitting in a saloon hoisting a few drinks.

Jim remarked: "My wife is the ugliest woman who was ever born."

"She can't be," replied Tom. "My wife is the ugliest woman you've ever seen."

They argued for about fifteen minutes, and Jim finally said, "Look, Tom—I'll bet you $100 that my wife is the ugliest woman you've ever come across." He removed a wallet from his pocket and took out her picture.

"Okay," Tom conceded. "She is ugly. Now come home with me and I'll show you my wife."

They walked to Tom's house, and Tom walked directly to his den. He rolled up the rug on the floor. Under the rug was a trap door. He lifted up the trap door and yelled into the darkness below, "Come on up, darling."

The wife replied, "All right, dear, I'm coming, but do you want me to put the bag over my head?"

"Not this time," Joe said. "I don't want to fuck you, honey. I just want to show you off."

Airline hostess: "Would you like some of our TWA coffee?"

Passenger: "No, thank you, but I'd love some of your TWA tea."

A young man, anxious for some sexual exercise, picked up a hot little number in Central Park, not realizing that she was a nymphomaniac. He took her to a hotel. After six times, she was screaming for more. After the seventh, exhausted, he slipped out of the room on the pretense of buying cigarettes. He stopped in the men's room, unzipped his fly, and couldn't find anything.

In a panic he reached inside his shorts. It was still there, but tiny and all drawn up. In a soothing voice he whispered, "It's all right. You can come out now. She's not here!"

The recruits for the college football team were lined up to take their first physical before the new coach and, of course, were stripped naked. Charlie, the candidate for the tight end job, stepped before the coach, who was amazed to see that Charlie's cock was about sixteen inches long but only half an inch thick.

The coach exclaimed, "Charlie, what the hell happened to you?"

Charlie explained, "Listen, I was nineteen years old before I found out you weren't supposed to roll it between your hands."

Stan did a hitch in the navy, which kept him away for eighteen months, during which his beautiful young wife sat at home awaiting his return.

On the first day of his leave she spied him entering their apartment house and quickly ran to the bedroom, throwing off all her clothes. She sat there breathlessly until she heard Stan's heavy knocking at the door.

"Darling," she yelled as she ran to fling it open, "I know why you're knocking."

"Yes," he gasped, "but do you know what I'm knocking with?"

The elderly couple, celebrating their golden anniversary, had a night on the town. After they prepared for bed the husband reached across the felt for his wife's hand.

"Not tonight, dear," she said, withdrawing her hand. "I'm too tired."

Abishop in a small Midwestern town bought two parrots and taught them to say the rosary. He even had two sets of tiny rosary beads made for them.

After months of exhaustive training, the parrots were able to recite the rosary and use the beads at the same time. The bishop was so pleased that he decided to teach another parrot the rosary. He went to the pet store and bought a female parrot, which he brought home and put into the cage with the other two.

As he did this, one parrot turned to the other and said, "Throw away your beads, George—our prayers have been answered!"

This is the true story of Cinderella, who was the most promiscuous bitch in the entire kingdom. She never said no. She never even said maybe. One day, the fairy godmother appeared and said, "Cinderella, you just have to stop screwing everybody who approaches you. You'll never be able to marry the prince unless you do."

Cinderella promised and tried her damnedest, but only a week after her talk with the fairy godmother she was caught in bed with the chimney sweep and his two assistants. The fairy godmother became so enraged that she changed Cinderella's pussy into a pumpkin!

Two weeks later, the fairy godmother, paying another visit to see how Cinderella was doing, caught her singing and dancing and smiling—a very happy girl. "Why are you smiling?" asked the fairy godmother.

"Because I've just met Peter Peter!" was the reply.

The customer in a bordello was dismayed to see the unshaven armpits of the hooker as she undressed.

"So much wool, so much wool!" he muttered.

As she slipped off her panties, he noticed another prodigious growth.

"So much wool, so much wool!" he exclaimed again.

The girl retorted, "Look, mister, did you come here to get laid or to knit?"

The dictionaries have different definitions, but we all know that an optimist says the glass is half-full while the pessimist sees it as half-empty. Others know that an optimist is a girl who doesn't take a pessimist with her on a cruise.

Girl in movie house: "The man next to me is masturbating!"
Girlfriend: "Ignore him."
"I can't; he's using my hand!"

Sam had been a soldier at war for more than three years, during which he had been in many battles and won many decorations. He was finally discharged from service and returned home to a wife and son whom he hadn't seen in almost four years.

As he was walking up the path to his house, his young son spotted him and yelled, "Mommy, Mommy, here comes Daddy, and he's got a purple heart on!" to which the mother replied, "I don't give a damn what color it is! Let him in, and you go play at the Joneses' for a couple of hours."

How do porcupines make love? V-e-r-y carefully!

Morris left for a two-day business trip to Chicago. He was only a few blocks from his house, when he realized that he had left the airplane tickets on his bureau top. He returned and quietly entered the house. His wife, in her skimpiest negligee, was standing at the sink washing the breakfast dishes.

She looked so inviting that he tiptoed up behind her, reached out, and squeezed her left tit.

"Leave only one quart of milk," she said. "Morris won't be here for breakfast tomorrow."

The new husband, a Cockney stagehand, had a most satisfactory nuptial night with his young bride. Forgetting his marital state he quickly dressed himself, threw several half-crowns on the bureau, and headed for the door. On the way out he recalled his new status and returned to his bride. There he found her biting on the coins in an experienced manner.

General Custer's troops had just come from a tremendous battle with the Indians in which the Indians were badly defeated. After the troops had left to return to the fort, the Indian chief called his tribe together and said, "I must report on the battle. There is good news and there is bad news. The bad news is that we were soundly trounced by the American troopers. They burned down our camp, raped our women, and took our food supplies. We'll have nothing to eat throughout this cold winter except buffalo turds."

The chief's son piped up: "If that's the bad news, what's the good news?"

The chief said, "There are plenty of buffalo out here."

What were the first words Eve used when she beheld Adam?

"Don't stick that thing in me!"

She snuggled up to him and murmured, "I'm yours for the asking. . . . I'm asking fifty dollars."

A stately-looking matron was walking through the Bronx Zoo, studying the animals. When she passed the porcupine enclosure she beckoned to a nearby attendant.

"Young man," she began, "do the North American porcupines have sharper pricks than those raised in Africa?"

The attendant thought a moment. "Well, ma'am," he answered, "the African porcupine's quills are sharper . . . but I think their pricks are about the same."

A kindly young woman saw a little boy standing on a street curb attempting to relieve himself. Giving in to her maternal instincts, the woman helped the lad release his organ from his pants. She evinced considerable surprise when the organ proved to be a man-sized tool, growing in her hand as the lad sighed with relief. "How old are you, little man?" she asked.

"Thirty-three, ma'am," answered the pint-sized jockey.

Papa," said the farmer's son, "you were a sheep-herder in your younger days; perhaps you can tell me where virgin wool comes from."

"Virgin wool, my son, comes from the sheep the herders couldn't catch."

Douglas was a bit of a nut who enjoyed making obscene phone calls. His biggest pleasure, however, was to make such calls to kindergarten teachers.

He'd find a lonely telephone booth, dial the number of some teacher, and exclaim, "Is this Mrs. Jones, the kindergarten teacher at P.S. 22?

"It is? Well, wee-wee, poo-poo, ca-ca!"

Girls who use their heads can stop the population explosion.

Joe was selling chance books for the Sacramental Softball and Social Society. During his first day's work, he came upon Mrs. Skettington, an old lady who lived on his block. He knocked on her door and said, "Mrs. Skettington, would you please buy some chances for the Sacramental Softball and Social Society?"

Mrs. Skettington answered, "I'm hard of hearing. What is that you're selling?"

"I'm selling chances for the Sacramental Softball and Social Society."

"What's that?" she said.

In disgust, Joe turned his back and walked away, muttering, "Fuck you, Mrs. Skettington," under his breath.

To which Mrs. Skettington answered, "Well, fuck the Sacramental Softball and Social Society!"

A whore's customer, deciding to leave without payment, yelled at the supine lady, "If it's a girl, call it Fatima."

"Fine," said the whore, "and if it's an itch, you call it eczema!"

The young farmer who had just taken a bride was concerned over his ability to perform on his nuptial night. When it came bedtime he attempted to exercise his conjugal duty, to no avail.

The next day he visited his local doctor and explained the problem. "The opening one customarily expects to find in a woman is missing," he said.

The doctor gave the matter much consideration and concluded that the bride must spend time with him. The farmer agreed, and the young bride repaired to the doctor's house

The next day the anxious husband inquired about results.

"Excellent results," said the doctor. "I labored and labored for hours with your wife. For a while I thought it was hopeless, but I am pleased to tell you that her love canal is now rosy and open and as slick as oil. Enjoy yourself, and my fee will be moderate."

The grateful farmer paid his bill.

Farmer Brown had been screwing one of his pigs for four years, when he was suddenly hit by pangs of conscience. It tortured him so much that he decided to tell the priest about it in confession.

The priest was shocked and could only say to Farmer Brown, "Well, tell me, was the pig a male or a female?"

"A female, of course," said Farmer Brown. "What do you think I am—some sort of a queer?"

Stanley was taking his very first airplane ride and had been so nervous that he had been plagued by constipation for a full week before the flight.

Finally flight day came, and after takeoff he felt so much better that he decided to move to the back of the plane and visit one of the lavatories.

While Stanley was having a hard time relieving himself, he heard the door to the adjacent lavatory open and close. He listened while a gentleman relieved himself loudly.

Stanley sighed through the thin partition: "I can tell that you were constipated too, but it's great to hear that you've been lucky."

To which the man replied: "It's a big relief, and it will be even better when I get my pants down!"

A concerned patient visited his physician and asked him if masturbation was harmful.

"No," the doctor said. "Not if you don't do it too often."

"How about three times a day?"

"That seems a little excessive. Why don't you get yourself a girl?"

"I've got a girl," the patient said.

"I mean a girl you can live with and sleep with."

"I've got one like that."

"Then why in heaven's name do you masturbate three times a day?"

"Oh," said the patient disgustedly, "she doesn't like it during mealtimes."

Jack was enthusiastic over the new girl he had found at the neighborhood massage parlor. "You like three-way broads," he told his friend. "Well, this one knows four ways."

"What's the fourth way?" asked his friend.

"She lets you go down on her."